BROWN PRIDE

BROWN PRIDE

Coach Greg Zavala

ISBN: Softcover   978-1-7960-6847-4
           eBook   978-1-7960-6846-7

Print information available on the last page.

Rev. date: 11/25/2019

To order additional copies of this book, contact:
Xlibris
1-888-795-4274
www.Xlibris.com
Orders@Xlibris.com
805012

AZTEC WARRIORS
BROWN PRIDE
CHOLA
HOME BOY
CHOLO
PACHUCO
ZOOTSUITERS
COLORING BOOK
AND HANDBOOK
CHICANA
CHICANO
PACHUCA
AUTHOR: GREGORY A. ZAVALA

CONTENTS

INTRODUCTION

Growing up in the south-side neighborhood in Tracy, California, we knew not to cross the tracks. Mexicans and other minorities lived on the south side, and of course white Americans lived on the north side.

During this time, African Americans were called Negros, and brown-skinned people were called Mexicans, even if we had been born in the United States.

I did grow up speaking Spanish instead of in English, but I was still born in America. The same was true for my mother and my mother's siblings.

During this time, there were some overtones of racial hatred toward some minority groups. Usually they were groups of color, such as Negros and Mexicans. As individuals and a group, we were often targeted by white Americans, who called

us names and degraded who we were. At times there were some physical altercations, especially among the young who defended their family and their culture.

The labels that started those fights included *wetback, bean eater, nigger,* or *boy.* The phrase that really angered people of color was "Swim back to Mexico (or Africa)"—even if the person in question had been born in the United States.

Now, in 2019, people of color are defending themselves again because President Trump, during his campaign for the presidency of the United States, called Mexicans and Hispanics murderers, rapists, gangsters, drug dealers, and illegal immigrants.

The purpose of this book is to give both people of color and those not of color insight into which people have contributed to making America great: the hard workers in agriculture, education, law enforcement, sports, business, government, medicine, and the military, among other industries. It is important to celebrate cultural differences in food, music, and traditions, such as the low-rider vehicles created by men and women of color.

Young people of color must remember where they came from; they are responsible for carrying on the traditions of their culture and the bloodline that helped their culture survive through the years. Some youth come from families of Aztec warriors or from Latino heroes such as Pancho Villa, Emiliano Zapata, and César Chávez. We must all remember to be brown and proud.

ANCIENT MEXICO

During the early times of ancient Mexico, the country was controlled by three different civilizations. There were three powerful tribes: the Acolhua people of Texcoco, the Mexica of the Tenochtitlan, and finally, the Tepaneca of Tlacopan. These groups together became known as the Aztec Empire, located in what is now modern Mexico.

The Mexica were the strongest and most powerful of all three tribes; they became the ruling tribe of the groups. All tribes agreed in matters of faith and politics.

During the sixth century, the first Nahuatl-speaking group came to live in Mexico. The Mexica had traveled into the area sometime between 1110 and 1248, trying to find a favorable place to live. They settled near a lake called Texcoco but did not live there long; they were forced out by the Tepanecas.

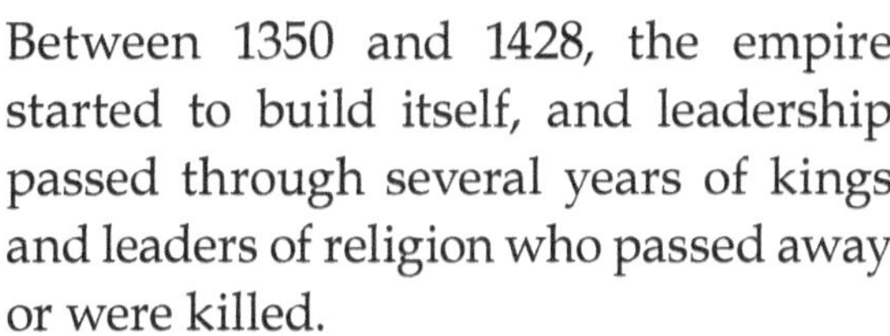

In 1299, Mexica had to get permission to settle on land of Tizapan. Cocoxtli of Culhuacan granted that permission. Tenochtitlan was settled by a new tribe in 1325.

Between 1350 and 1428, the empire started to build itself, and leadership passed through several years of kings and leaders of religion who passed away or were killed.

In 1430, war broke out between Mexica and Tepaneca. Mexica lost the confrontation, and they moved to a new location called Azcapotazalco.

A new ruler arose named Itzcoatl, and his empire lasted from 1427 to 1440. After thirteen years, he stepped down from the throne.

In 1440, Moctezuma I became the new emperor of Mexico. In 1469, major changes in leadership took place. In 1492, the most famous ruler of all kings took control of the empire, Moctezuma II.

During this period, the Aztecs had several enemies, one of which they could not overrun or conquer. The Tarascan people, led by King Cazonc, were as strong as the Aztecs.

The fall of the Aztec Empire came when Captain Hernán Cortés of Spain landed in Yucatan and traveled to Tenochtitlan in 1519.

Cortés went to war against the Aztecs with the help of Tlaxcala, their hostile rivals. In the battle called La Noche Triste ("The Sad Night"), the Spanish Conquistadores and Tlaxcala warriors were defeated. They both suffered heavy losses among their warriors.

In 1521, Cuauhetemoc lost Tenochtitlan to Cortés, who destroyed the city and renamed it in Spanish, Mexico City, and declared it the capital of New Spain.

The last emperor of Tenochtitlan was tried and sentence to death by the conquistadors, the new rulers of New Spain, in 1525.

MEXICO INDEPENDENCE
SEPTEMBER 16, 1810
"El Grito de Dolores"

The next chapter of *Brown Pride* is how Mexico obtained its own identity and independence from Spain.

There were several heroes who started the revolution to free the people of Mexico. The first was a European who visit the homeland of Mexico. His name was Francisco Hernández de Córdoba, and he landed on the Yucatan Peninsula in 1517 from a small island Cuba.

When de Córdoba landed with a small force of Spanish explorers, they met with natives of the land and were forced to return to Cuba.

In 1519, Cuban governor Diego Velázquez Cuéllar fought back with a larger force under the leadership of Hernán Cortés. Cortés and his forces were able to conquer the Aztec Empire.

Changes in Spain's control start to take place in 1810, almost three hundred years after their arrival. One of the heroes who wanted a change and started the early fight against Spanish control was Father Miguel Hidalgo, who is famous for "El Grito (Cry) de Dolores," which gained support and action from thousands of natives and mestizos in the small village.

Before the revolt of "El Grito de Dolores," there were small rebellions toward Spanish colonial government control.

The translator for Hernán Cortés, La Malinche, was one of those who led the fight. Her son, Martín Cortés, known as El Mestizo, was fathered by Hernán Cortés.

These small revolts included people called Criollos, those of near or full Spanish descent. The issue they focused on was the exclusion of human and political rights.

By 1808, France had taken control of Mexico, and the Spanish colonies there began to fall. That when Father Hidalgo's "El Grito de Dolores" occurred. But in 1811, the priest was killed, and new faces entered the picture for Mexican independence. General Agustín de Iturbide and Vicente Guerrero led a new path toward Mexico's independence in 1814.

In 1821, Iturbide and Guerrero developed and released the Plan of Iguala. It was designed to give Mexico its independence under the control of a monarchy, and the Catholic Church would oversee equal rights and upper-class status for the Spanish and Mestizo population. In addition, the Treaty of Córdoba was signed that year, forcing Spain out of Mexico.

In 1833, General Antonio López de Santa Anna became president of Mexico; he stopped Spain, who tried to recapture the country.

In the Battle of San Jacinto in 1844, Santa Anna was defeated by Sam Houston and was forced to resign.

In 1846, Mexico's land was of great interest to the United States, and it declared war against Mexico. US forces invaded Mexico City in 1847, led by General Winfield Scott; they captured the city and its people.

The war ended with the Treaty of Guadalupe Hidalgo, a signed agreement between Mexico and the United States. The United States did purchase three states—present-day Texas, California, and New Mexico. The United States paid $15 million for all three, cutting Mexico's territory in half.

NEW WARS OF MEXICO
1861-1923

Benito Juárez was a Zapotec Indian who became a new leader after a series of revolts and the restructuring of Mexico's debts. President Juárez took steps to stop payments to other countries, such as France, Great Britain, and Spain.

Juárez was then chased out of Mexico City by Napoleon III's forces of France, and Maximilian von Habsburg became emperor of Mexico in 1861.

In 1867, France removed its troops from Mexico after a Mexican general, Porfirio Díaz, and his troops invaded Mexico City and arrested and hanged Maximilian. Díaz reinstated Juárez as president of Mexico.

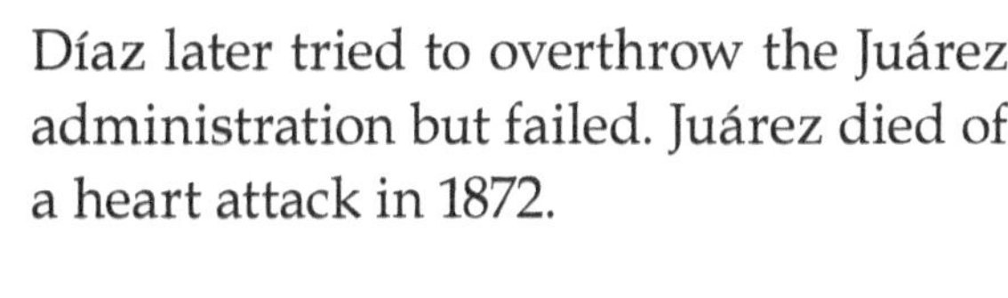

Díaz later tried to overthrow the Juárez administration but failed. Juárez died of a heart attack in 1872.

Porfirio Díaz led another revolt in 1877, which succeeded. He rebuilt the commercial and economic status of Mexico. His plan brought in foreign investors such as the United States and Great Britain.

Mexico City became a financial giant, but the only ones who benefited from the new structure were the upper class. The changes left the poor out of wealth and political reform, which led to inequality for the poor population and another revolt.

Francisco Madero, a well-educated lawyer, tried to unseat President Díaz in 1910. Madero became the new voice for the poor, and another revolt began.

Madero wrote the Plan of San Luis de Potosí, which pushed for major changes in the Mexican government. He wanted to instill a democracy, federalism, agrarian reform, and workers' rights, and he declared war on the Díaz administration. Díaz stepped down in 1911, but Madero still had a country with a decade's worth of problems.

During the Madero presidency, two heroes of the working class and peasants led a new revolt. From southern Mexico came Emiliano Zapata, and from northern Mexico came Pancho Villa.

In 1913, Madero was overthrown by one of his own generals, Victoriano Huerta, who then became president of Mexico. Villa, Zapata, former president Díaz, and Venustiano Carranza forced Huerta to resign in 1914.

Carranza took the power and the presidency of Mexico, and Zapata and Villa continued their revolt against Carranza.

1910-1914
WOMEN OF THE MEXICAN REVOLUTION
SOLDADERAS

ADELITAS

Names to remember:

Petra "Pedro" Herrera
María Quinteras de Meras
Angela "Ángel" Jiménez
Amelio Robles Ávila

It is important to note that women of the revolution played a vital part in the revolt and independence of Mexico.

During this period, they were called *soldaderas* and *adelitas*.

The women were responsible for taking care of the wounded, cooking, cleaning, setting up camps, and seeing that their weapons were in working condition.

Some of the women became officers for Zapata and were promoted to leadership roles, some as high as colonels leading two hundred men.

They were an important element of the Mexican revolution. It's not to say that there was any justice from Villa or Zapata, but those women survived and became a crucial part of the revolutionary armies.

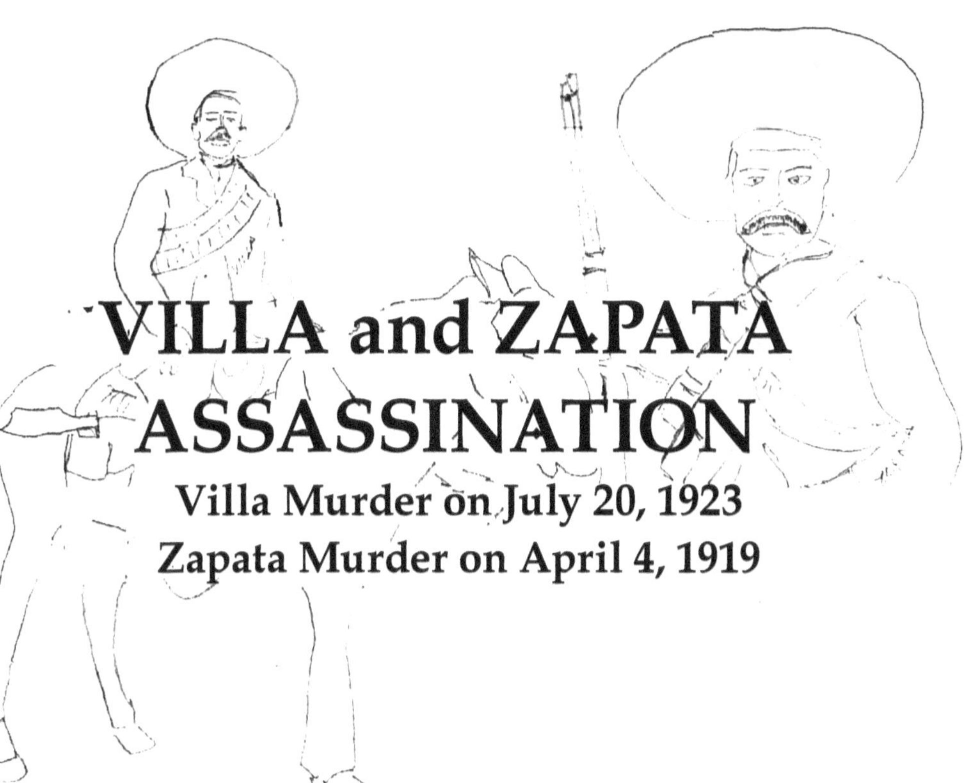

VILLA and ZAPATA ASSASSINATION

Villa Murder on July 20, 1923
Zapata Murder on April 4, 1919

Pancho Villa

José Doroteo Arango Arámbula
June 5, 1878–July 20, 1923

Many people of Mexico consider Pancho Villa a revolutionary hero. Prior to his fame, he was a young man who worked on lands belonging to landlords.

At age thirteen, he killed Agustín López Negrete for disrespecting his sister. That incident made him an outlaw. He took refuge in the Sierra Madre and joined other bandits. Villa became very skillful in handling weapons and horses. But a greater attribute was his leadership ability and skill at gaining the trust of peasants.

In 1910, Madero asked Villa to help overthrow the Díaz presidency. Madero became president but was murdered by Huerta.

In 1913, Villa joined with Zapata and Carranza to take Huerta out of the office. In 1914, he parted ways with Carranza, the new president of Mexico.

Villa attacked Columbus, New Mexico, because President Wilson betrayed him and supported Carranza.

In 1920, Villa made a deal and retired to a hacienda in northern Mexico.

In 1923, Villa was set up to be murdered on the streets of Parral, Chihuahua. The prevailing theory is that the murder was payback for his war crimes.

In a sad case, Villa's grave was later robbed for money.

Emiliano Zapata
Emiliano Zapata Salazar
August 8, 1879–April 10, 1919
Zapata's famous revolutionary cry:
"I would rather die on my feet
than live my whole life
on my knees!"

Emiliano Zapata was very popular in the southern parts of Mexico. He was known as a man of the people.
His goal was to give the peasants of southern Mexico ownership of a piece of land so they could have good lives and farms.

This was a struggle between Zapata and the landowners.

In 1910, Zapata joined forces with Madero to get President Díaz out of office, with the understanding that his people would get their land.

In 1911, the Battle of Cuautla occurred; it was a six-day fight that broke down Díaz's government and forced him to flee Mexico.

Madero then took over the presidency of Mexico. He had promised Zapata that he would give the peasants their land, but he changed his mind and kept Díaz's policies.

Zapata then distanced himself from Madero and drafted a plan to remove him from office. Known as the Plan of Ayala, it indicated that Madero was unfit to be president.

In 1913, General Victoriano Huerta became the president of Mexico and had Madero murdered. Huerta then resigned in 1914, and Venustiano Carranza became president.

It was President Carranza who ordered the murder of Emiliano Zapata in 1919. Some, however, believe that Zapata lived to a ripe old age.

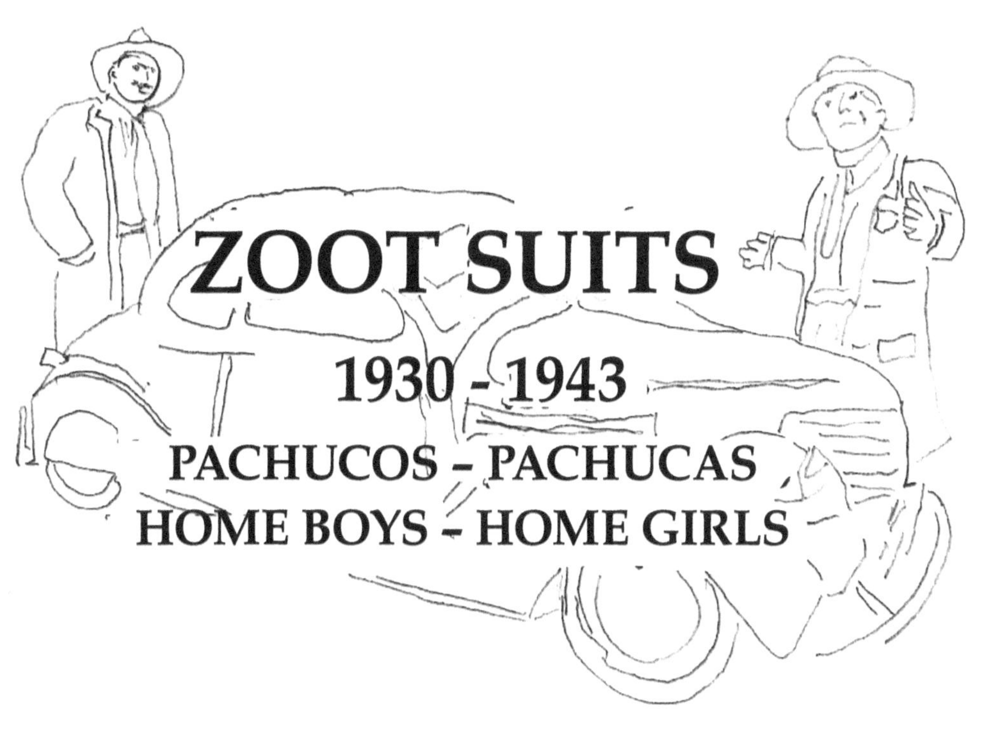
ZOOT SUITS
1930 - 1943
PACHUCOS - PACHUCAS
HOME BOYS - HOME GIRLS

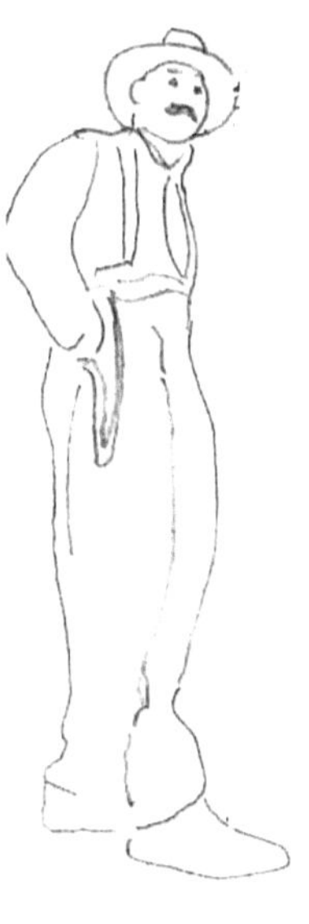

In my research, I encountered several events of the past that seem to be repeating themselves in the present time. One of those events relates to the issue of skin color, culture, and language.

As stated, President Trump of the United States has made comments that have made people of Latino descent angry and afraid to be part of America. In 2016, during his run for president, Trump stated in his speech that Mexico was to blame for the problems that the United States was having with drug dealers, murderers, and rapists. In addition, those Mexicans crossing the border were also taking jobs from white Americans. He said, "We need to build a wall to keep them out." What Trump fails to realize is that people of Latin American countries help America become great.

Yes, people of color do have problems within in our culture … but so do other cultures. But what Trump did not do is state that there are people of color who are loyal, dedicated, and honorable. And those people make great contributions toward making America great.

We as a people have had many challenges while living in this country we now call home. Many people of color joined US forces to fight and defend the red, white, and blue flag during World War II and in Korea, Vietnam, Iraq, and Afghanistan. Many gave their lives, and we have a president who calls those people of color criminals.

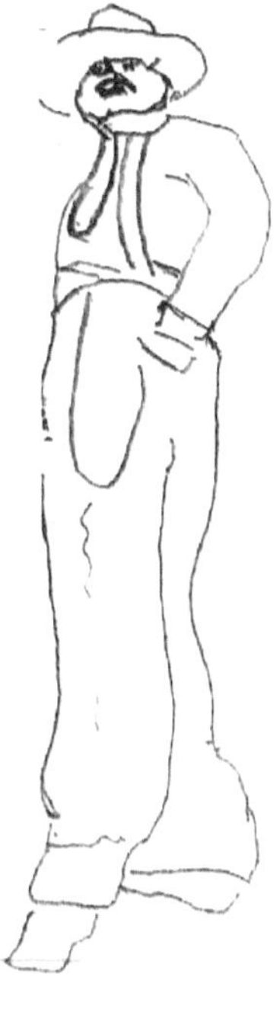

At the present, many men and women who served in the US military are being deported back to their birth countries. Many people joined the military to obtain citizenship. And this is how they are treated.

We are repeating events that happened during the 1930s and 1940s. The Zoot Suit Riots occurred in 1943 in Southern California. They involved people of color, mostly Mexican Americans.

Most people of Mexican descent who moved to the United States settled in several states. During the Mexican Revolution, many people ran from the war and its dangers to live across the border.

In 1942, the United States entered World War II. American and Mexican men and women joined together to fight the Axis powers (Germany, Italy, and Japan). It was during this time that the United States and Mexico made an agreement to allow men of Mexico to cross the border and work for the United States. This was the bracero program, initiated in 1942.

During this time, there was a fashion explosion of zoot suits from the East Coast, starting in black Harlem in the 1930s. Young Mexican American men adopted the zoot suits. White America could not understand the movement and believed it was a type of criminal behavior.

In 1943, there was a clash between US military personnel and young zoot suiters. Basically, the cause was that these young men were buying cloth that made the suits. The military servicemen believed that the material was needed to make military uniforms. Well, it can be said that was one of the problems. And racial tensions between the groups started to grow.

The *LA Times* did not help the situation. This was when the terms *pachucos* and *pachucas* were used to identify young Mexican men and women.

What was disheartening was that law enforcement personnel just stood by and let military servicemen attack anyone wearing a zoot suit. Their victims were not only Mexican American, but also African Americans and Filipino Americans.

The riots lasted several days and stopped when US military personnel were denied leave from the barracks.

The governor of California at the time, Earl Warren, put together a committee to investigate what caused the riots. The committee found that it was racial prejudice.

Today Mexican Americans celebrate the zoot suit era.

THE TIME OF CHANGE
1960 – PRESENT

Political Movements for the People of Color

VIVA LA RAZA

BROWN POWER

The sixties were years of racial challenges and change. The Black Panthers fought for civil rights and human rights. They made changes in education, health, and political systems. Following in their footsteps was a group called the Brown Berets, founded in 1960 by Carlos Montes. Their purpose was also to fight the US government's racial suppression and injustice.

In addition to other movements among people of color, United Farm Workers erupted on the scene in the 1960s. The organization was led by César Chávez, who spearheaded strikes against grape growers, vegetable growers, fruit orchards, and farmers.

César's actions were aimed at improving working conditions and wages for field workers and migrants throughout California. He led several protest marches that included one special political figure, Robert Kennedy. Cesar did win for the people: Latinos, Blacks, and Filipinos.

During this period, people of color encountered other issues, such as the military draft and the Vietnam War. That war was highly protested in the United States. Military forces pulled out years later, in 1971.

There were other tragedies during this time period. President John F. Kennedy was murdered on November 22, 1963, in Dallas, Texas. The president's brother Robert Kennedy was murdered in Southern California on June 6, 1968. The brothers were considered the people's choices.

BLACK PANTHER POWER

TWIN TOWERS

A more recent tragic event was the terrorist attack on the Twin Towers of the World Trade Center in New York City. The towers opened on April 4, 1973, and were destroyed on September 11, 2001, by terrorists on two airlines flights.

This sad event pulled American people of all colors together to fight terrorism. We as a nation stood together to fight terrorism.

Then for the first time, the United States elected an African American president. Barack Obama was the forty-fourth president of the United States. He served two terms, from January 20, 2009, to January 20, 2017. His popularity among the people of the United States was high through his presidency.

Things became worse in 2016, when Donald Trump decided to run for president. His campaign focused on attacking people of color and the Muslim religion. His first targets were people

of Latino decent and undocumented immigrants—especially people of Mexico, whom he referred to as murderers, drug dealers and rapists. In addition, he promised white Americans that he would build a wall to keep them out and that Mexico was going to pay for it.

President Trump has made vulgar remarks about people, countries, and religions. He has gone so far as to say they should go back to where they came from, especially people of Muslim religion and those from Africa. His remarks have caught the ears of nationalist groups and hate groups, who are strong supporters of his policies against people of color.

PEOPLE of AMERICA UNITED

CON GANAS SI PUEDES!

In the United States of America, there are many DREAMers who live throughout the nation. They have contributed to this great country and are continuing to do so. Mr. Trump wants to deport them because their parents are not American citizens and they are here illegally. One real issue is that some of these immigrants have served in the military and have fought in the Middle East.

Upon their return from their tours of duty, they are deported and not given US citizenship as the government has promised. Some of these military personnel have given their lives to serve America. This is how they are treated by this president.

Martin Luther King Jr. believed in a nonviolent approach during the civil rights movements in the sixties. He once said that people should not be judged because of the color of their skin, the language they speak, or the country they came from. They should be given the opportunity to be accepted as human beings who can make the United States great. Martin Luther King Jr. was assassinated on April 4, 1968, the same year as Robert Kennedy. We as a nation lost great leaders of human rights.

We are people of pride and character. Continue to reach for goals in life, and treat people like you would like to be treated.